Alfred's

Music for Little Mozarts

Written Activities and Playing Examples to Reinforce Note-Reading

The *Notespeller & Sight-Play Book 4* reinforces note-reading skills based on the concepts introduced in the *Music Lesson Book 4*. The pages in this book correlate page by page with the materials in the *Music Lesson Book*. They should be assigned according to the instructions in the upper right corner of the pages in this book. They also may be assigned as review material at any time after the students have passed the designated *Music Lesson Book* page.

Each page of the *Notespeller & Sight-Play Book* has two activities—a written activity and a playing example. The written activity reinforces notes on the keyboard and the staff through coloring, circling, drawing, or matching. The sight-play examples help students:

• Relate notes and musical concepts to performance on the keyboard.

• Move out of fixed hand positions.

• Identify melodic and rhythm patterns.

For the sight-play examples, teachers may use the following preparation steps:

❶ Clap (or tap) the rhythm and count aloud evenly.

❷ Point to the notes and rests and count aloud evenly.

❸ Play and say the finger numbers.

❹ Point to the notes and say the note names.

❺ Play and say the note names.

Alfred

Alfred Music
P.O. Box 10003
Van Nuys, CA 91410-0003

Illustrations by Christine Finn

No part of this book shall be reproduced, arranged, adapted, recorded, publicly performed, stored in a retrieval system, or transmitted by any means without written permission from the publisher. In order to comply with copyright laws, please apply for such written permission and/or license by contacting the publisher at alfred.com/permissions.

Christine H. Barden · Gayle Kowalchyk · E. L. Lancaster

Copyright © 2016 by Alfred Music
All rights reserved.   Printed in USA.
ISBN-10: 1-4706-3242-X
ISBN-13: 978-1-4706-3242-7

Use with Alfred's Music for Little Mozarts, Lesson Book 4, page 5.

Review: Notes in C Position

Help the music friends review notes in C Position.
Draw a line connecting the dots to match the notes to their letter names.

D–E–C

G–F–E

E–F–G

E–C–D

Sight-Play

C POSITION

Play and count.

mf

Count: 1   1   1   1   1   1   1   1 – 2

Review: Melodic Intervals

Draw a line connecting the dots to match the notes to their melodic interval name.

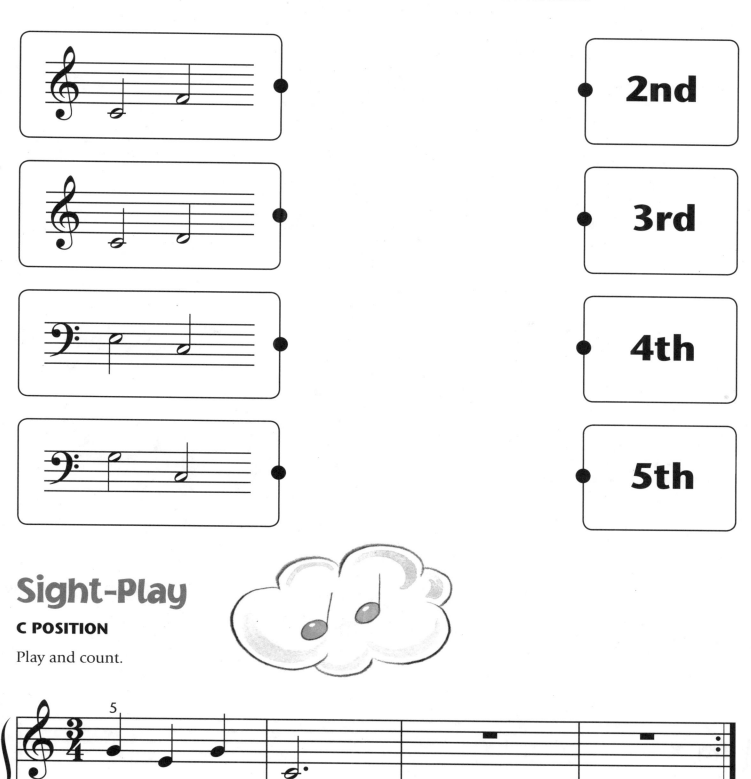

Sight-Play

C POSITION

Play and count.

Count: 1   1   1   1 – 2 – 3

Use with page 7.

Review: Harmonic Intervals

Help Nannerl Mouse, Mozart Mouse, and J. S. Bunny find the harmonic intervals.
Circle each harmonic interval with a **red** crayon.

Sight-Play

C POSITION

Play and count.

Count: 1 – 2   1 – 2

Review: Hands Together in C Position

Help the music friends name notes that are played hands together.
Circle the correct note names.

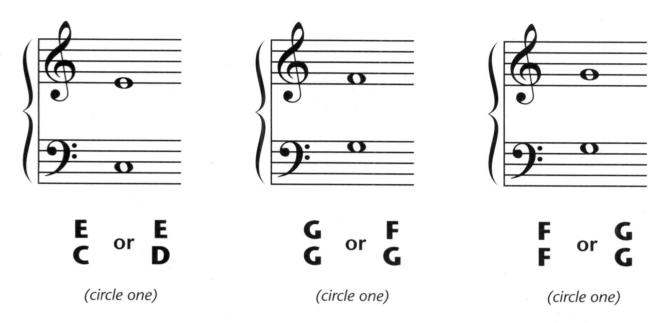

E   E
C   or   D

(circle one)

G   F
G   or   G

(circle one)

F   G
F   or   G

(circle one)

Sight-Play

C POSITION

Play and count.

Count: 1 – 2 – 3   rest

Use with page 10.

Review: Hands Together in Middle C Position

Help the music friends name notes that are played hands together.
Circle the correct note names.

E or D
B   B

(circle one)

E   E
F or G

(circle one)

G or F
C   C

(circle one)

Sight-Play

MIDDLE C POSITION

Play and count.

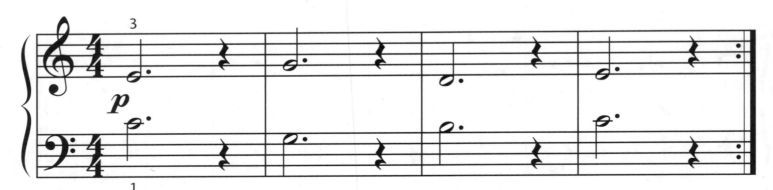

Count: 1 – 2 – 3   rest

Review: Notes in Middle C Position

Help Clara Schumann-Cat review notes in Middle C Position.
Draw a line connecting the dots to match the notes to their letter names.

D–F–E

F–A–C

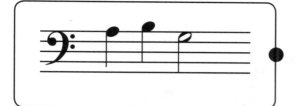

G–E–C

A–B–G

Sight-Play

MIDDLE C POSITION

Play and count.

Count: 1   1   1   1   1 – 2 – 3

8

Use with page 15.

A in Treble Clef

Pachebel Penguin just found space note A.
Trace the A whole notes.

Sight-Play

Pachelbel Penguin wants you to try this funny trick.
Use different RH fingers to play space note A.

Play and count.

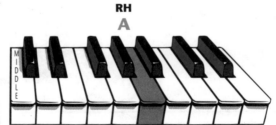

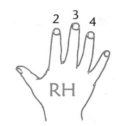

Count: 1 – 2   rest

B in Treble Clef

Nannerl Mouse just found line note B.
Trace the B whole notes.

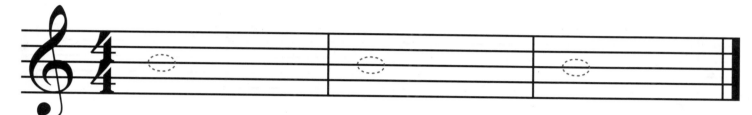

Sight-Play

Nannerl Mouse wants you to try this funny trick.
Use different RH fingers to play line note B.

Play and count.

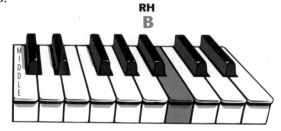

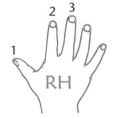

Count: 1 – 2   rest

Use with page 17.

Low G in Bass Clef

Mozart Mouse just found line note Low G.

Trace the Low G whole notes.

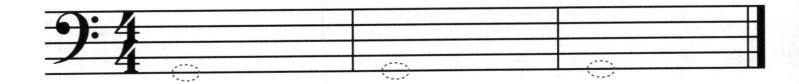

1. Circle Treble G with a **red** crayon.
2. Circle Bass G with a **blue** crayon.
3. Circle Low G with a **green** crayon.

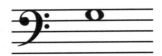 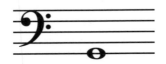 

Sight-Play

Mozart Mouse wants you to try this funny trick.
Use different LH fingers to play line note Low G.

Play and count.

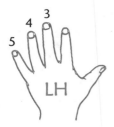

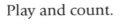

Count: 1 — 2   rest

Low A in Bass Clef

Professor Haydn Hippo just found space note Low A.
Trace the Low A whole notes.

Sight-Play

Professor Haydn Hippo wants you to try this funny trick.
Use different LH fingers to play space note Low A.

Play and count.

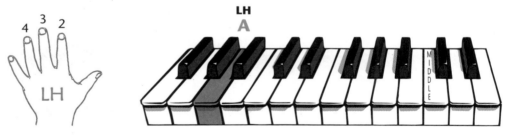

Count: 1 – 2 rest

Use with page 19.

Low B in Bass Clef

Professor Haydn Hippo just found line note Low B.
Trace the Low B whole notes.

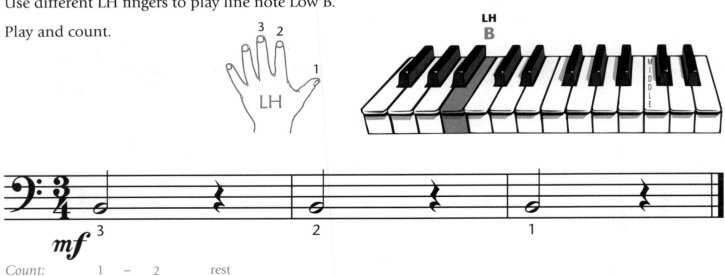

Sight-Play

Professor Haydn Hippo wants you to try this funny trick.
Use different LH fingers to play line note Low B.

Play and count.

Count: 1 – 2   rest

C in Treble Clef

Nina Ballerina and Mozart Mouse just found space note Treble C.

Trace the Treble C whole notes.

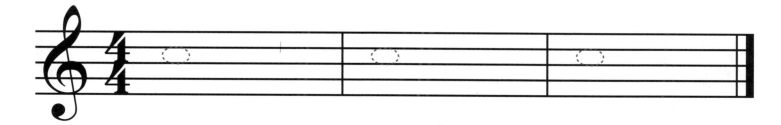

1 Circle Middle C with a **purple** crayon.

2 Circle Treble C with a **green** crayon.

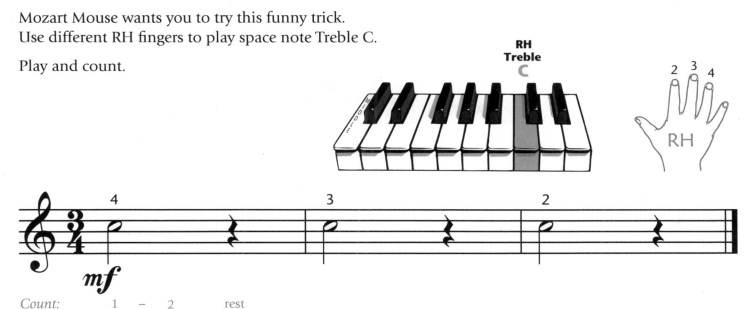

Sight-Play

Mozart Mouse wants you to try this funny trick.
Use different RH fingers to play space note Treble C.

Play and count.

Count: 1 – 2   rest

Use with page 21.

D in Treble Clef

Puccini Pooch just found line note Treble D.

Trace the Treble D whole notes.

1. Circle Bass D with a **brown** crayon.
2. Circle Middle D with a **blue** crayon.
3. Circle Treble D with a **green** crayon.

Sight-Play

Puccini Pooch wants you to try this funny trick.
Use different RH fingers to play line note Treble D.

Play and count.

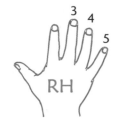

Count: 1   –   2   rest   –   2

G Position in Treble Clef

Draw a line connecting the dots to match each note to its letter name.

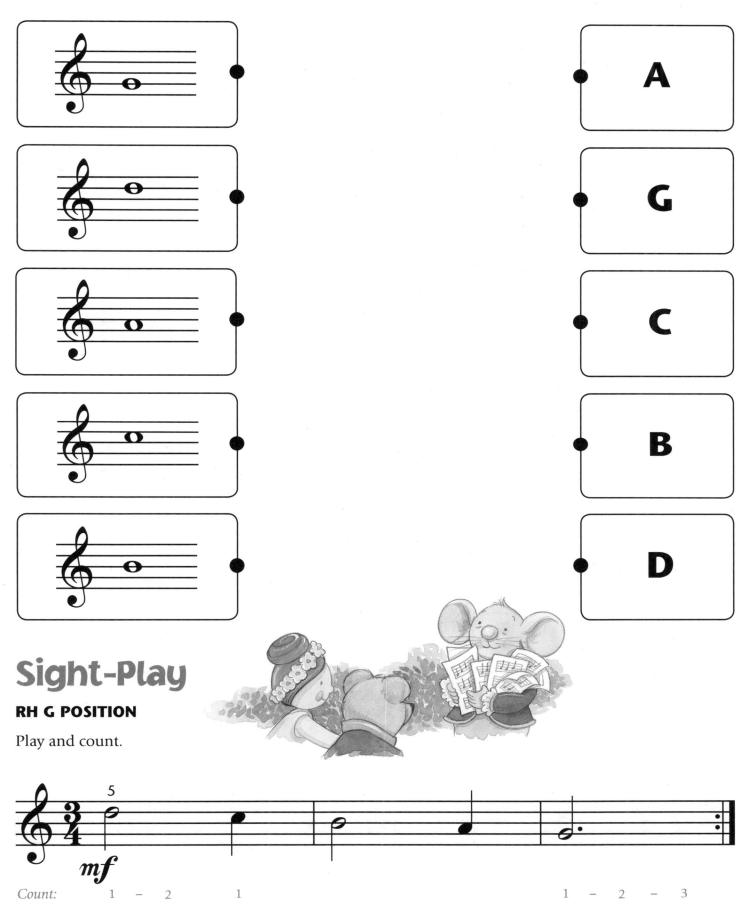

Sight-Play

RH G POSITION

Play and count.

Count: 1 – 2 1   1 – 2 – 3

Use with page 24.

Intervals in RH G Position

Draw a line connecting the dots to match the notes to their interval name.

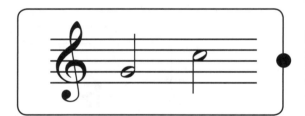

2nd

3rd

4th

5th

Sight-Play

RH G POSITION

Play and count.

Count: 1 – 2   1 – 2   1 – 2 – 3 – 4

G Position in Bass Clef

Draw a line connecting the dots to match each note to its letter name.

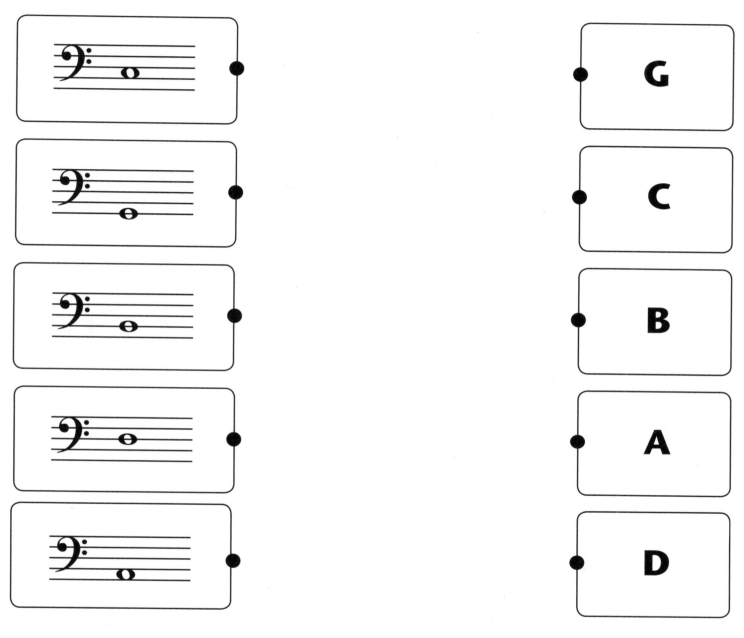

Sight-Play

LH G POSITION

Play and count.

18

Use with page 27.

Intervals in LH G Position

Draw a line connecting the dots to match
the notes to their interval name.

2nd

3rd

4th

5th

Sight-Play

LH G POSITION

Play and count.

mf ⁴⁄₅

Count: 1 – 2   1 – 2   1 – 2 – 3 – 4

Hands Together in G Position

The audience will cheer when you name the notes that are played hands together.
Circle the correct note names.

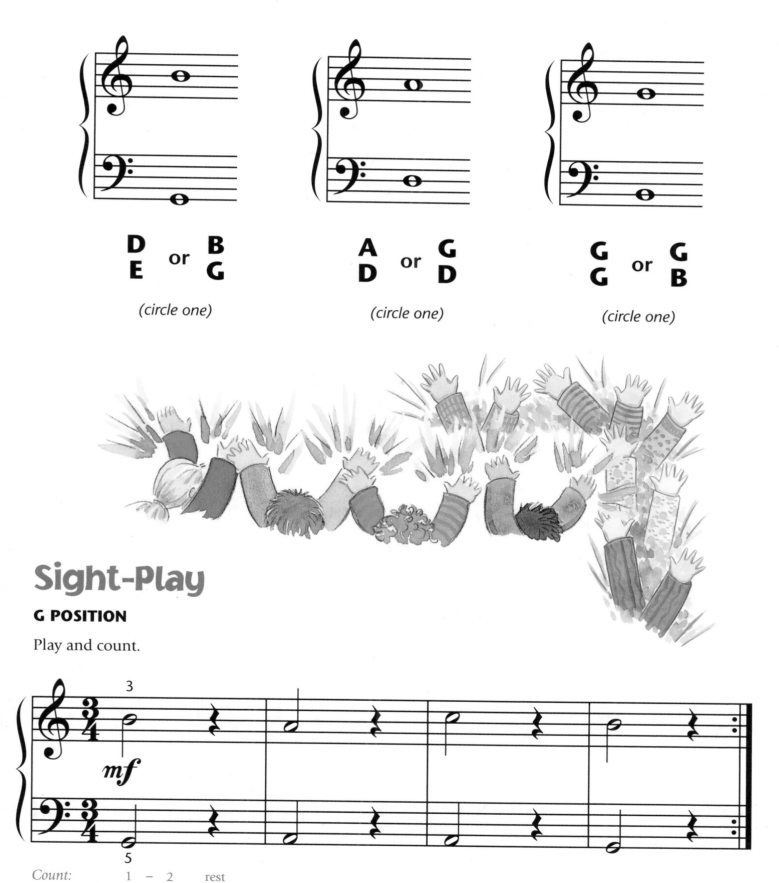

D
E or **B**
         G

(circle one)

A
D or **G**
         D

(circle one)

G
G or **G**
         B

(circle one)

Sight-Play

G POSITION

Play and count.

Count: 1 – 2 rest

Harmonic and Melodic Intervals in G Position

Help Nannerl Mouse and Mozart Mouse find the harmonic intervals.

1 Circle each harmonic interval with a **blue** crayon.

2 Circle each melodic interval with a **yellow** crayon.

Sight-Play

G POSITION

Play and count.

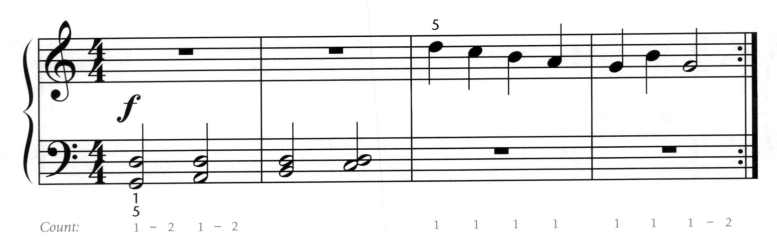

Count: 1 – 2   1 – 2   1   1   1   1   1   1   1 – 2

Flat Sign

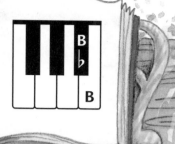

Help the music friends find B♭ on the keyboard.
Circle each B♭.

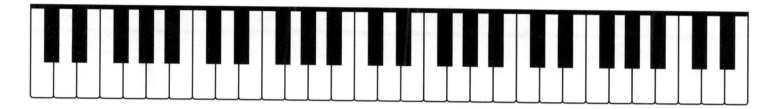

Sight-Play

G POSITION (with B♭)

Play and count.

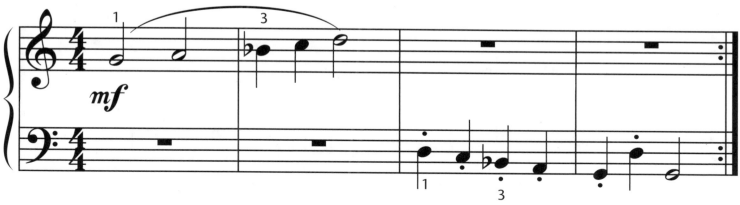

Count:　　1 - 2　1 - 2　　1　1　1 - 2　　1　1　1　1

Use with page 31.

Finding E♭

Help the music friends find E♭ on the keyboard.
Circle each E♭.

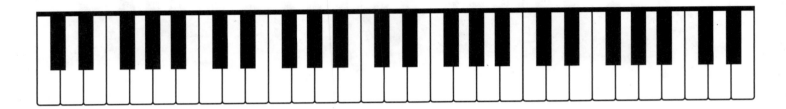

Sight-Play

C POSITION (with E♭)

Play and count.

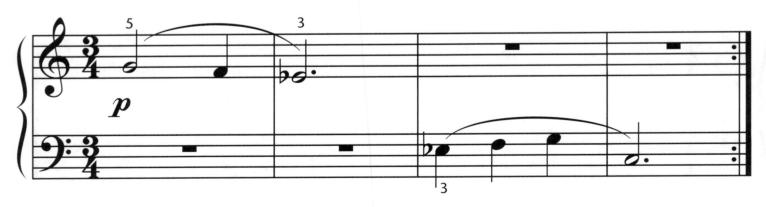

Count: 1   –   2   1   1   –   2   –   3   1   1   1

More About Flats

1 Draw a line to connect each note in treble clef to its matching keyboard.

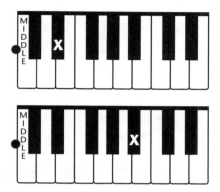

2 Draw a line to connect each note in bass clef to its matching keyboard.

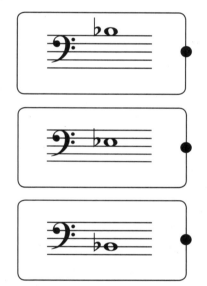
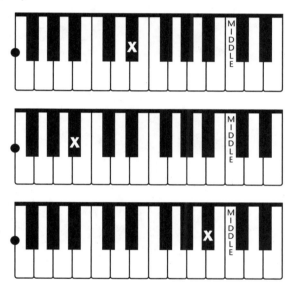

Sight-Play

MIDDLE C POSITION (with B♭ and E♭)

Play and count.

Count: 1 – 2   1 – 2   1   1   1 – 2   1   1   1   1   1 – 2 – 3 – 4

Sharp Sign

Use with page 33.

Help the music friends find F♯ on the keyboard.
Circle each F♯.

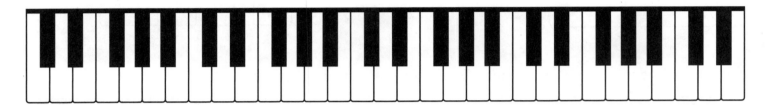

Sight-Play

C POSITION (with F♯)

Play and count.

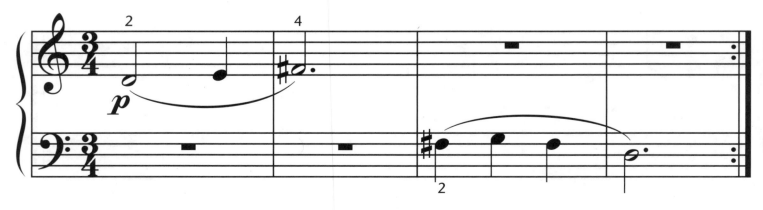

Count: 1 – 2   1   1 – 2 – 3   1   1   1

Finding D♯

Help the music friends find D♯ on the keyboard.
Circle each D♯.

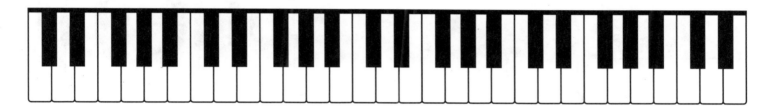

Sight-Play

MIDDLE C POSITION (with D♯)

Play and count.

Count: 1   1   1   1   1 – 2   1 – 2

26

Use with page 35.

More About Sharps

Draw a line to connect each note
to its matching keyboard.

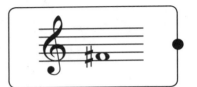

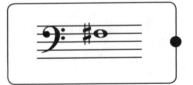

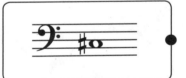

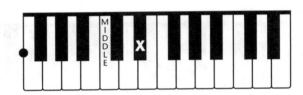

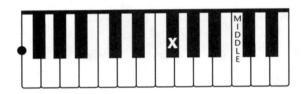

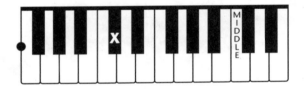

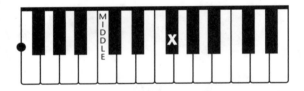

Sight-Play

G POSITION (with C♯)

Play and count.

Count: 1   1   1 – 2   1   1   1   1   1

Tied Notes

Help Beethoven Bear and Mozart Mouse name the tied notes.

Circle the correct note names.

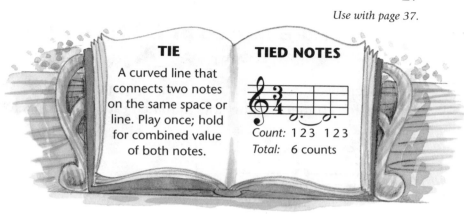

TIE

A curved line that connects two notes on the same space or line. Play once; hold for combined value of both notes.

TIED NOTES

Count: 1 2 3   1 2 3
Total: 6 counts

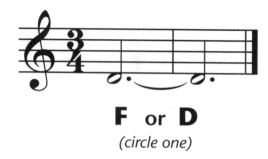

F or **D**
(circle one)

E or **G**
(circle one)

D or **F**
(circle one)

C or **A**
(circle one)

Sight-Play

MIDDLE C POSITION (with B♭)

Play and count.

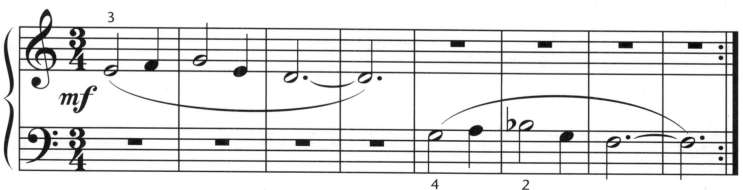

Count: 1 – 2   1   1 – 2 – 3 – 1 – 2 – 3

Use with page 39.

Review: Note Names in Treble Clef

Help Beethoven Bear and Mozart Mouse name the notes.
Draw a line connecting the dots to match each note to its letter name.

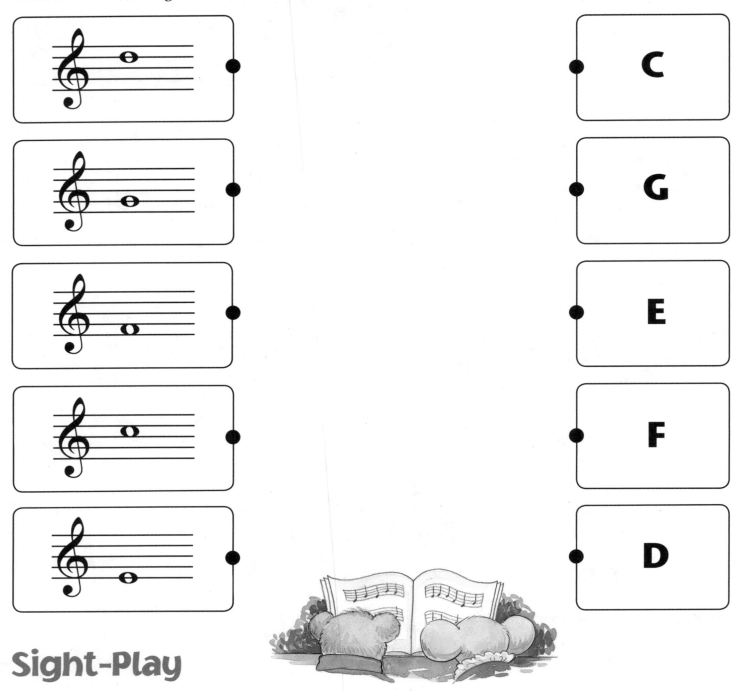

Sight-Play

Beethoven Bear and Mozart Mouse want you to try this funny trick.
Move to a new RH position during the rest.

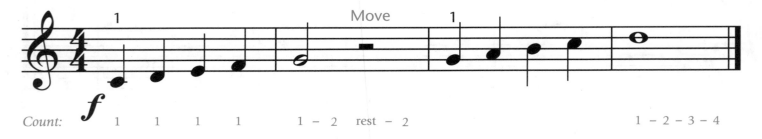

Review: note names in Bass Clef

Draw a line connecting the dots to match each note to its letter name.

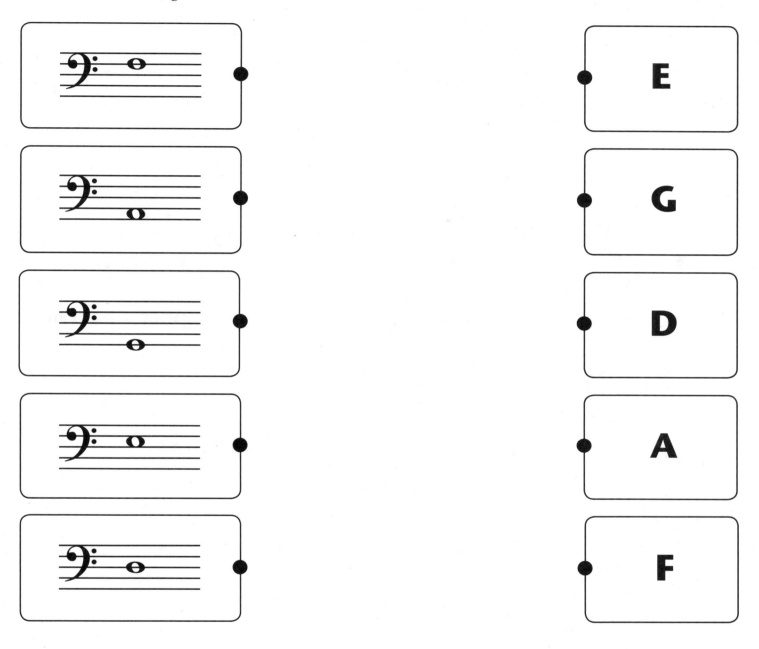

Sight-Play

Puccini Pooch wants you to try this funny trick.
Move to a new LH position during the rest.

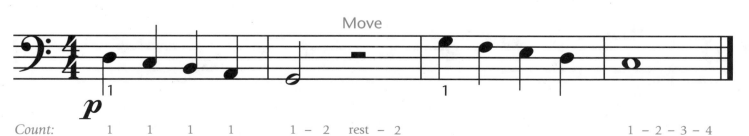

Use with page 41.

Crescendo and Diminuendo

C POSITION
or
G POSITION
(circle one)

MIDDLE C POSITION
or
C POSITION
(circle one)

MIDDLE C POSITION
or
C POSITION
(circle one)

1 Circle the name of each position.

2 Draw a line to connect each position that gets gradually louder to the book with the *crescendo* sign.

3 Draw a line to connect each position that gets gradually softer to the book with the *diminuendo* sign.

Sight-Play

The music friends want you to try this funny trick.
Move to a new LH position during the rest.

Play and count.

Move

Count: 1   1   1   1   1 – 2   rest – 2   1 – 2 – 3 – 4

Review: Harmonic Intervals

Draw a line connecting the dots to match the notes to their interval names.

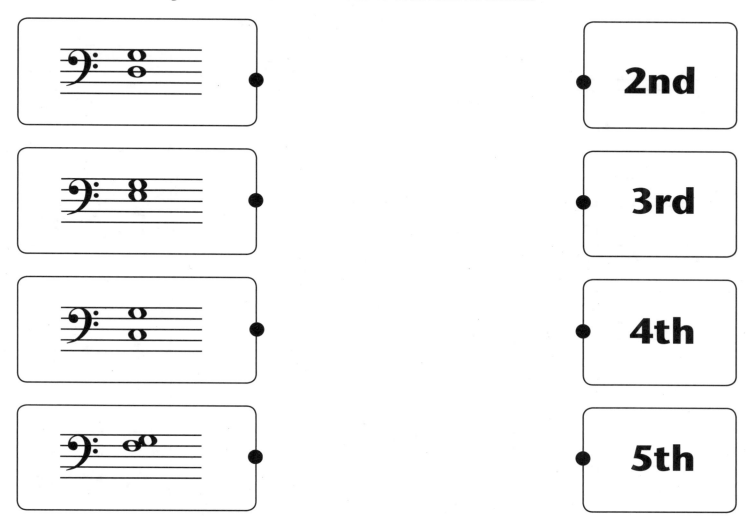

Sight-Play

Mozart Mouse wants you to try this funny trick. Move to a new LH position during the rest to play the harmonic intervals.

Play and count.

Review: Note Names

Draw a line connecting the dots to match the notes to their letter names.

Use with page 47.

C–E–G

C–A–B

F–D–E

G–D–B

Sight-Play

MIDDLE C POSITION

Play and count.

Count: 1 – 2   1 – 2   1   1   1   1   1 – 2 – 3 – 4